CANNES
The Delaplaine 2020 Long Weekend Guide

Andrew Delaplaine

GET 3 FREE NOVELS
Like political thrillers?
See next page to download 3 FREE page-turning novels—no strings attached.

**NO BUSINESS HAS PAID A SINGLE PENNY OR GIVEN *ANYTHING*
TO BE INCLUDED IN THIS BOOK.**

A list of the author's other travel guides, as well as his political thrillers and titles for children, can be found at the end of this book.

Senior Editors - ***Renee & Sophie Delaplaine***
Senior Writer - **James Cubby**

Gramercy Park Press
New York – London – Paris

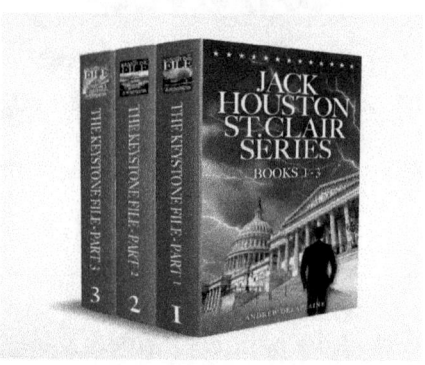

WANT 3 FREE THRILLERS?

Why, of course you do!

If you like these writers--
Vince Flynn, Brad Thor, Tom Clancy, James Patterson, David Baldacci, John Grisham, Brad Meltzer, Daniel Silva, Don DeLillo

If you like these TV series –
House of Cards, Scandal, West Wing, The Good Wife, Madam Secretary, Designated Survivor

> You'll love the **unputdownable** series about Jack Houston St. Clair, with political intrigue, romance, and loads of action and suspense.

Besides writing travel books, I've written political thrillers for many years that have delighted hundreds of thousands of readers. I want to introduce you to my work!

Send me an email and I'll send you a link where you can download the first 3 books in my bestselling series, absolutely FREE.

Mention **this book** when you email me.

andrewdelaplaine@mac.com

Copyright © by Gramercy Park Press - All rights reserved.

Cannes
The Delaplaine Long Weekend Guide

TABLE OF CONTENTS

Chapter 1 – WHY CANNES? – 7

Chapter 2 – GETTING ABOUT – 10

Chapter 3 – WHERE TO STAY – 12
*High on the Hog – Sensible Alternatives
On a Budget*

Chapter 4 – WHERE TO EAT – 22

Chapter 5 – NIGHTLIFE – 49

Chapter 6 – WHAT TO SEE & DO – 57

Chapter 7 – SHOPPING & SERVICES – 61

INDEX – 73

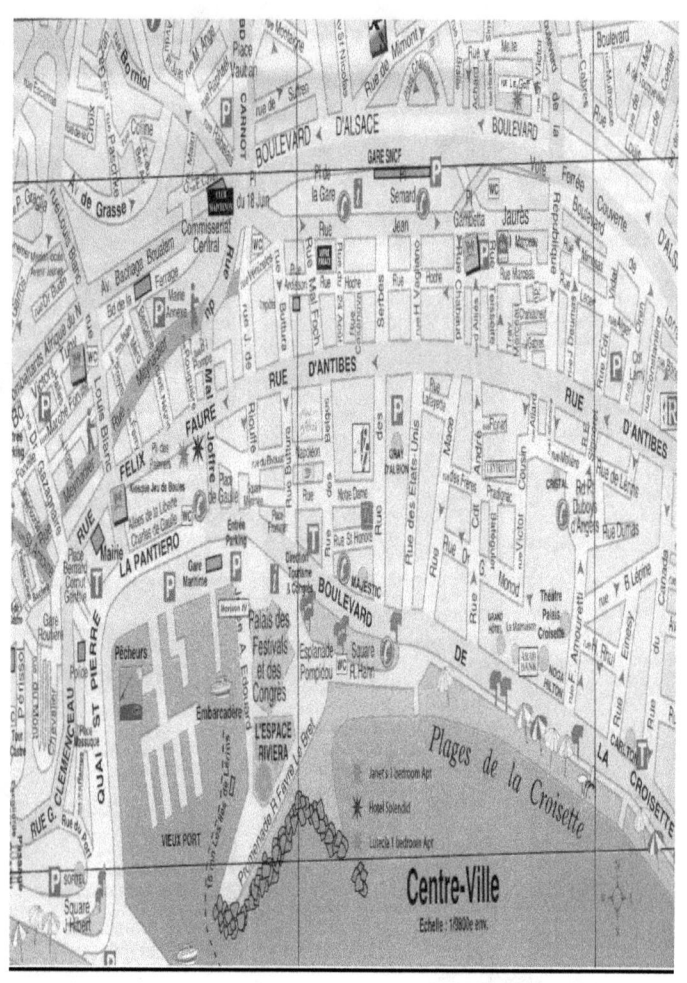

Chapter 1
WHY CANNES?

Although people associate Cannes with the film festival that takes place here every May, a good thing to remember about Cannes is that this is perhaps the one month you'll want to avoid the city.

Either way, it's one of the jewels of the Riviera and has to be seen once in your life.

It's as much fun in winter as in summer, in spring as in fall. Every time I visit (I'm in the movie business also, so it's usually in May that I'm there), I wonder what I'm doing living somewhere else when this place is available. There's just nothing like it in the world.

It's got superior weather, lots of interesting historical attractions, stunning beaches with the tranquil Mediterranean waters lapping the shoreline, all manner of outdoor activities associated with the water: sailing, fishing, swimming, yachting.

Cannes also has fine shopping, in the same manner as Worth Avenue in Palm Beach does. The Cartier store may not be that big, *but it's there*, just in case an Arabian potentate or South American ex-pat dictator may stroll in to buy a bauble for his mistress-of-the-week. (And they do, believe me.)

Another good thing about Cannes is that it's so centrally located, right on the main rail line running from Marseille right through Nice to Monte Carlo and then into Italy.

Cannes. How to pronounce it properly? Americans usually mispronounce it by giving it what they think is a "French" sound, *CON* or *CAHN*. The proper way to say it is simpler than you think. It's exactly like the English word *CAN*.

Chapter 2
GETTING ABOUT

Public transportation has never been a problem in Cannes. Wherever you need to go, there is always a way to get there. There is a convenient train system that takes you from city to city along the Riviera. An added benefit of this train system is that you get to enjoy the beautiful scenery of the along the coast. One thing that will strike you is the abundance of flowers. There are everywhere, surrounding architectural historic monuments, houses, city fountains, houses and restaurants. How many cities in the U.S. do you see so tastefully planted?

BUSES

Within the city, the bus system will take you just about anywhere. Hop on any of them. It's one a Euro. Need a pass? No problem. They have those as well. The **Carte 10 pass** gives you 10 rides at reduced rates. Be alert to the fare you purchase, as some fares are expensive.

The buses run every 15 minutes ore so, depending on traffic.

TAXIS

Taxis are available. Hail one on the street or call to have one come to you: **Taxis de Cannes** at +33 (04) 929-9272. Fares are pre-set by the city, and after an initial charge of a couple of euros, the fare increases at the rate of €3.00 per mile, so it can be a little costly.

Chapter 3
WHERE TO STAY

CARLTON
58 boulevard de la Croisette, Cannes, 33-4-9306-4006
www.intercontinental.com
Nothing says "Cannes" better than the Carlton. As I say elsewhere in these pages, go inside the lobby, have a drink or two and take in the splendor. This lobby (both the bar and the **Carlton Beach Restaurant**) is ground zero for deal-making during the film festival. But long before the movie business changed the nature of the clientele, this classic Belle Époque hotel has been a seaside destination for the most discriminating

guests for over a century. Walk down the Croisette and you'll pass the best in designer shops. The luxury suites overlook the Mediterranean Sea, and island boat trips are easily arranged. There's a fitness center open 24/7 where you can work off those rich meals you're destined to eat while visiting this town. Every other possible amenity is available here.

CHATEAU SAINT-MARTIN AND SPA
2490 Avenue des Templiers, Vence, +33 4 93 58 02 02
www.chateau-st-martin.com
A 12th-century Knight Templar Castle featuring plush rooms with scenic views of the Mediterranean Sea up in the hills of Vence. From here you can see from the Italian border all the way down to St. Tropez. Amenities include: Complimentary Wi-Fi, flat-screen TVs and marble bathrooms. This unique chateau/spa has a heated swimming pool, restaurant **(even if you don't stay here, try to work in a visit to the restaurant—it's really wonderful),** a fitness center, an oak-paneled bar, tennis courts, a posh spa, and access to a private beach. The beautiful grounds include gardens and terraces of the chateau. Note: no internet access and no pets. Non-smoking rooms available. Located near Chapelle du Rosaire de Vence, a church designed by Henri Matisse, and the Musée Renoir. Wine tasting from the chateau's extensive wine cellars.

THE FIVE SEAS HOTEL
1, rue Notre Dame, Cannes, 4-63-36-05-05
www.fiveseashotel.com/
This ultra-modern place is a recent addition to Cannes. It's right next to the Palais des Festivals and only has 45 rooms; this is the perfect boutique hotel for a trip to Cannes. You'll love the bright, airy hip design with upbeat cheerful colors and modern furniture designs. There's a tea room here, the **SALON DE GOURMANDISES**, where the pastries are out of this world, created by Chef Jérôme De Oliveira, one of the best pastry chefs in the world. There's also a trendy restaurant on site, the **SEA SENS**, up on the fifth floor. Nice view. Also a rooftop pool and lounge where you can have drinks.

HOTEL 3.14
5, rue Francois Einesy, Cannes, 330-49-70-63-69
www.314cannes.com
Another new alternative to the big old majestic hotels here in Cannes. This one has 5 floors, and each floor is designed to reflect the cultural ambience of one of the 5 continents, Africa, Oceania, etc. They even claim that the ancient techniques of Feng Shui have been employed in the design to promote good circulation. (They even have classes in Feng Shui.) A fun, lively place to stay.

HOTEL BARRIERE LE MAJESTIC
10 Boulevard de la Croisette, Cannes, +33 4 92 98 77 00
www.hotelsbarriere.com
Beautiful legendary hotel offering 350 guestrooms and suites. Amenities include: Complimentary Wi-Fi,

flat-screen TVs, and minibars. Luxury suites come with butler service. Hotel facilities include: outdoor pool, on-site restaurant, gym, private beach, and private projection room. Located on the Croisette, this hotel offers beautiful views of the Mediterranean Sea. Pet-friendly.

VILLA GABRES HOTEL
62, Boulevard Alsace, Cannes, 4-93-46-66-00
www.villagarbo-cannes.com
Just a few feet behind the Croisette is this building from 1884 that used to be the Hotel de Gabres. They kept the Beaux-Arts exterior, but entirely revamped the inside into a modern hotel, but still small as they rechristened it the **Villa Garbo**. They offer 11 large apartments on 3 floors, so you'll feel like you're

living here rather than renting as room. Complete line of luxury services, including a Spa. Breakfast every morning and an open bar from 6-8 every night. In the winter, it's inside their lounge by a white marble fireplace. In summer, it's outside on their palm-lined terrace.

HOTEL DU CAP-EDEN ROC
Boulevard JF Kennedy, Antibes, +33 4 93 61 39 01
www.hotel-du-cap-eden-roc.com
This 1870 luxury landmark hotel features three buildings with 116 elegant guestrooms, many with courtyard views. Amenities include: complimentary Wi-Fi, flat-screen TVs, and marble bathrooms. Hotel features include: onsite bar/grill, fine-dining restaurant, spa, outdoor pool, 5 tennis courts, and a kids' club. One of the most desirable settings on the Côte d'Azur.

HOTEL LE CANBERRA
120 Rue d'Antibes, 06400 Cannes, +33 4 97 06 95 00
www.hotel-cannes-canberra.com/
NEIGHBORHOOD: Centre-ville
The lobby of this 4-star hotel offers a relaxing refuge from the hustle and bustle of the street outside. The lounge bar is open 24/7, so it's always a nice place to grab that final nightcap of the evening. They have 30 guest rooms and 5 suites decorated with trendy 1950s-style furnishings. Amenities: Complimentary Wi-Fi, flat screen TVs, and minibars. Hotel features: On-site restaurant for fine dining **Le Café Blanc**, featuring a menu with Mediterranean cuisine, cocktail lounge, heated outdoor pool, exercise room and sauna. Located on the main shopping street Rue d'Antibes, and just 5 minutes from La Croisette.

HOTEL PRULY
32, Boulevard d'Alsace, Cannes, 4-93-38-41-28

www.hotel-pruly.com
In an elegant whitewashed townhouse you'll find this charming inn with a dozen or so rooms. Each room has a name: Josephine, Louise, Pauline, etc., and while they're smallish and very Spartan, it's nice, quiet, comfortable, affordable and beautifully located.

RADISSON BLU 1835 HOTEL & THALASSO
2 Boulevard du Midi Jean Hibert, Cannes, +33 4 92 99 73 00
www.radissonblu.com/en/hotel-cannes
Located at the base of the historic district, this chic hotel offers 134 elegant rooms and suites. But the standout feature is the stunning view old the Old Port you'll get from the rooftop. Amenities include: complimentary Wi-Fi, alarm clocks, flat-screen TVs and minibars. Hotel facilities include: luxury spa with 46 treatment rooms, indoor/outdoor heated saltwater pool, whirlpool, hammam, steam rooms, health food restaurant and a fitness center. Other perks include: a private beach, a rooftop restaurant and bar with a panoramic view. Just a ten-minute walk from Palais des Festivals et des Congrès.

Chapter 4
WHERE TO EAT

AL CHARQ
20 Rue Rouaze, Cannes, +33 4 93 94 01 76
www.alcharq.com
CUISINE: Lebanese
DRINKS: Full bar
SERVING: Lunch & Dinner
PRICE RANGE: $$
Beautiful Lebanese eatery offering a varied menu with dishes such as hummus, chicken skewers and lamb. Of course the also serve falafels and an assortment of kebabs. Reservations recommended. Outdoor seating – weather permitting. Second lounge offering theme nights including live music and dancing.

ASTOUX ET BRUN
27 Rue Félix Faure, Cannes, +33 4 93 39 21 87

www.astouxbrun.com
CUISINE: Seafood
DRINKS: Beer & Wine Only
SERVING: Lunch/Dinner/Late Night
PRICE RANGE: $$$
Unfussy tavern type eatery offering a simple menu of seafood, and only a block from the Marché Forville. I think it's been here for decades. Fresh oysters, sea snails, and Sea Bass – all prepared simply and delicious. If it's seafood and you want it, they will have it on this menu. Nice outdoor seating on a quaint street under umbrellas. Or sit inside. Favorites: Stew of the sea and Scallop/crab risotto. There's something about the succulent sautéed scallops that's very special. These babies melt in your mouth. Nice wine list. Gluten free options. Nice selection of French wines. For dessert try the fresh apple tart with salted caramel ice cream. Locals' favorite, extremely noisy and packed. Like me, you'll love it.

CANNELLE
32 Rue Des Serbes, Le gray D'albion, Cannes, 4-93-38-72-79
www.cannelle-cannes.com
Salmon tartare with fries and a green salad makes a good lunch here in this open, floor-to-ceiling glassed-in spot. (There's an inside room as well.) The breakfasts are good as well. The ham, cheese & tomato omelette is great, and they make their own quiche here daily. The pastries aren't to be overlooked, either: I'm still telling people about the raspberry tarte I had here.

BIJOU PLAGE
Square Verdun, Boulevard de la Croisette, 93-45-31-50
www.bijouplagecannes.com
CUISINE: Seafood, Regional
DRINKS: Full Bar
SERVING: Lunch & Dinner
PRICE RANGE: $$$
The menu here ranges far and wide. Good value for the money. It is a very cozy restaurant and great view of the beach. Since the portions are so large, we decided to share a grilled beef rib for two with sauce béarnaise. Absolutely succulent.

COSY BOX
24 Rue Latour-Maubourg, +33 6 01 03 54 48
www.cosy-box.com
CUISINE: French
DRINKS: Full Bar
SERVING: Dinner, Late Night
PRICE RANGE: $$$$
Pop-up restaurant with an ever-evolving tasting menu of fine French cuisine near the Hotel Martinez. (When it's not Cosy Box, it's La Chunga restaurant.) Great selection of wines, champagnes and spirits.

CRESCI
3, Quai St Pierre, Cannes, 4-93-39-22-56
www.maison-cresci.fr
CUISINE: Pizza
DRINKS: Beer & Wine Only
SERVING: Lunch & Dinner

PRICE RANGE: $$
This company actually has a chain of restaurants running down the Riviera, but every time I'm here, I think it's the only one in the world. The pies here are quite large, so get just a small one.

GASTON ET GASTOUNETTE
6 Quai Saint-Pierre, Cannes, 93-39-49-44
www.gaston-gastounette.fr
CUISINE: Seafood
DRINKS: Full Bar
SERVING: Lunch & Dinner
PRICE RANGE: $$$$
Defnitely one of the best places in town for seafood. They have the more familiar Bouillabaisse, but there's a similar dish you might want to try: Bourride. It's like a Bouillabaisse, but they only use white fish in it.

GRILL & WINES
5 rue Notre Dame, 06400 Cannes, +33 4 93 38 37 10
www.grillandwines.com
CUISINE: Bistro/French
DRINKS: Beer & Wine Only
SERVING: Lunch & Dinner; closed Sundays
PRICE RANGE: $$
NEIGHBORHOOD: Cote d'Azur
Tucked behind the Hotel Majestic Barriere is this typical French bistro specializing in beef. They have created an elegant atmosphere and you can watch them work in the open kitchen. Their specialty – Fillet de Boeuf with green pepper sauce. Favorites: Duck Risotto and Pork Tenderloin with mushroom sauce. Nice wine selection. Outdoor seating available.

L'AFFABLE
5, rue Lafontaine, Cannes, 4-93-68-02-09
www.restaurant-laffable.fr
CUISINE: Mediterranean, Seafood
DRINKS: Full Bar
SERVING: Dinner
PRICE RANGE: $$$
With so many restaurants going overboard to show off the palm-lined streets of Cannes, it's nice to find an intimate, classy and windowless room where the focus is on the food and wine. Leather, wood, glass, marble, beige and brown tones basically sum up the décor. Clean lines, modern decor, but still very sophisticated. Ravioli with foie gras and morel sauce; cod brandade; sliced roast beef with herbs of Provence. Go for the Grand Marnier soufflé for dessert.

L'AME
Five Seas Hotel
1 Rue Notre Dame, +33 6 12 09 14 13
http://fiveseashotel.com/en
CUISINE: American/French
DRINKS: Full Bar
SERVING: Dinner, Late Night
PRICE RANGE: $$$$
Pop-up chic restaurant located on rooftop terrace restaurant of the centrally located Five Seas Hotel. Entertainment and top-notch cuisine. The bartenders here come from Le Perchoir, the trendy rooftop bar in Paris. If you're on a budget, come up for a drink, take in the view and then get the hell out before you break the bank.

L'ASSIETTE PROVENCALE
9 Quai Saint-Pierre, 33 4 93 38 52 14
www.assiette-provencale.fr
CUISINE: Provencal
DRINKS: Wine
SERVING: Lunch & Dinner
PRICE RANGE: $$$
NEIGHBORHOOD: Le Suquet
Popular indoor-outdoor eatery known for their Mojitos. Menu offers prix-fixe or a la carte options. Get the fish soup if they have it the day you're there. It's excellent. Favorites: Lobster Spring roll and Carpaccio of Smoked Salmon (they make this in-house). Save room for the Lemon Meringue Pie – it will not disappoint.

L'ECRIN PLAGE
Port Piere Canto
Boulevard de la Croisette, +33 4 93 43 43 33
www.ecrinplage.com
CUISINE: French/Mediterranean/Asian
DRINKS: Full Bar
SERVING: Dinner, Lunch (Tues – Sat)
PRICE RANGE: $$$
Located on the beach, great spot to dine overlooking the sea. Perfect for late in the afternoon, as it's at the Palm Beach end of the Croisette, away from most of the madness. Menu picks: Excellent pastas, Caesar salad and Sesame seared duck. Nice selection of wines. Have a pre-dinner cocktail on the deck while waiting for your table.

L'ONDINE PIAGE
64 Boulevard de la Croisette. Cannes, +33 4 93 94 23 15
www.ondineplage.com
CUISINE: French/ Mediterranean/European/Seafood
DRINKS: Full bar
SERVING: Breakfast, Lunch, Dinner, and Late Night
PRICE RANGE: $$$
Known as the only restaurant in Cannes with a beach, this eatery offers an extensive menu. One of the most popular eateries on the Croisette. Menu favorites: Grilled quail and Langustino and Mango salad. Reservations recommended.

LA BROUETTE DE GRAND-MERE
9 Bis Rue d'Oran, 33 4 93 39 12 10
www.labrouettedegrandmere.fr

CUISINE: French
DRINKS: Full Bar
SERVING: Dinner
PRICE RANGE: $$
NEIGHBORHOOD: Le Suquet
Yet another cuter-than-cute Bistro popular with locals (with indoor and outdoor seating) serving classic French fare family style. Only 5 dishes on the prix-fixe menu (check these out on the blackboard) but it's a variety of chicken, meat or fish. Favorites: Rabbit if they have it, always done nicely here; Lamb & potatoes and Homemade pate.

LA CASA DI NONNA
41 rue Hoche, +33 4 97 06 33 51
www.lacasadinonna.fr
WEBSITE DOWN AT PRESSTIME
CUISINE: Italian/Bistro
DRINKS: Beer & Wine Only
SERVING: Breakfast, Lunch, and Dinner; Closed Sun
PRICE RANGE: $$$
Specialty eatery offering up creative Italian cuisine. Perfect breakfast or lunch spot. Fresh juice bar. Favorites: Avocado toast, Vegetarian orecchiettes peas & zucchini and Veggie salad with quinoa. Save room for desserts like Apple/rhubarb pie.

LA CAVE
9 rue de la Republique, Cannes, 93-99-79-87
www.lacavecannes.com/
CUISINE: Seafood, French
DRINKS: Beer & Wine only

SERVING: Lunch & Dinner
PRICE RANGE: $$$

This local restaurant is great for seafood, but even more interesting are the specialties they have from Southwestern France. You might begin with the superior "tomato cake" that comes with a savory tapenade, or the ravioli in a pecorino sauce with truffles. The confit de canard was deliciously prepared, crispy and juicy. The sweetbreads in a morel sauce were lovely. The desserts such as the apple omelette and the strawberry soup with vanilla ice cream made our day. Simply delicious.

LA COLOMBE D'OR
1, place du General de Gaulle, St-Paul-de-Vence, 4-93-32-80-02
www.la-colombe-dor.com
CUISINE: Mediterranean
DRINKS: Full Bar

SERVING: Breakfast, Lunch & Dinner
PRICE RANGE: $$$$

By all means I urge you to go a bit out of town (about a half hour north of Cannes) to the charming village of St-Paul-de-Vence. Take your lunch here on the terrace and look out over the terraced hills and vineyards and gardens. See the same view Orson Welles and Yves Montand saw when they stayed here. (In fact, Montand married Simone Signoret in this place.) Dozens of internationally famous artists used to hang out here, from Picasso to Chagall. The food is classic Provençal family-style cuisine perfectly prepared and served in a setting so perfect you might want to cry. (By the way, if you're exploring the rest of Provence, you might want to consider staying here—they offer 13 rooms and 12 suites. A little pricey, but what the hell, right?)

LA GUERITE
Ile Sainte-Marguerite, +33 4 93 43 49 30
www.restaurantlaguerite.com
CUISINE: French/Mediterranean/European
DRINKS: Full Bar
SERVING: Dinner, Lunch (Tues – Sat)
PRICE RANGE: $$$$

Upscale dining experience with good music. You can hide away from the surging crowds on the Croisette by taking a short boat ride over to the Ile Sainte-Marguerite and have a bite at this lovely place. Even if you don't stop at this expensive restaurant, the extraordinary views from the island are worth the trip alone. Seafood creatively prepared is the emphasis here. Favorites: Lobster and Sea Bass. Live singers and musicians most nights and live DJ other times. This place attracts hipsters and fashionistas.

LA LIBERA
17, rue du Commandant Andre, Cannes, 4-92-99-00-19
www.restaurant-libera.com/
CUISINE: Italian
DRINKS: Beer & Wine Only
SERVING: Lunch & Dinner
PRICE RANGE: $4
Small little eatery that is just the spot if you want a break from French food; here you'll get authentic Italian cuisine at reasonable prices in a charming setting. For pizza, I like the one with mussels, tomato, garlic and parsley or the Sicilienne, with tomato, anchovies, capers and olives. It's not just pizza here, mind you, but a full range of great salads, meats and fish selections and other pasta dishes as well, my favorite among them being the veal Bolognese.

LA MEISSOUNIERE
15 Rue du 24 Août, 33 4 93 38 37 76
www.lameissouniere.com
CUISINE: French, Mediterranean
DRINKS: Full Bar
SERVING: Breakfast, Lunch, Dinner
PRICE RANGE: $$
NEIGHBORHOOD: Le Suquet
Located in the heart of the Cannes shopping district, this little eatery with a blackboard menu offers modern French cuisine in a simple atmosphere. Nothing fancy. If you like liver, you know how rarely

you see it on menus these days. They carry a lovely Grilled Calf's liver here. Favorites: Salmon tartare; Grilled Andouillette sausages with mustard; Duck breast served with a 'secret' sauce. Excellent selection of wine.

LA MOME
6 rue Florian, +33 4 93 38 60 95
http://lamomecannes.com
CUISINE: Italian/French/Mediterranean
DRINKS: Full Bar
SERVING: Dinner, Lunch (Tues – Sat)
PRICE RANGE: $$$
Popular eatery specializing in Italian and Mediterranean cuisine made with fresh seasonal products. Excellent raw bar attracts a buzzy crowd. It's tucked away on a quiet pedestrian street, but it's still close to everything. Menu picks: Beef carpaccio and Truffle risotto. Generous portions. Extensive cocktail menu.

LA PALME D'OR
Hotel Martinez
73 Blvd de la Croisette, Cannes, 92-98-74-14

https://hotel-martinez.hyatt.com/en/hotel/dining/la-palme-dor.html
CUISINE: French
DRINKS: Full Bar
SERVING: Lunch & Dinner
PRICE RANGE: $$$$

It is a unique sensory and culinary experience. Rated 2 Michelin stars and 4 toques by Gault & Millau. Pretty much the ultimate French dining experience with excellent service surrounded with a beautiful view of the Bay of Cannes and the Mediterranean Sea. Thin slices of venison with iodized seeds, wild mushrooms ice cream; roasted filet of shoulder marinated for 48 hours, finished off with with fruits, salty foie gras topped on a sweet potato pulp with hazelnut in a pepper sauce. Oysters carpaccio style with shallots and vinegar, brioche, duck foie gras, citrus zests.

LA PLAGE RESTAURANT
HOTEL BARRIERE
10 Boulevard de la Croisette, Cannes, +33 4 92 98 77 30
www.hotelsbarriere.com/en/cannes/le-majestic.html
CUISINE: French/European/Mediterranean
DRINKS: Full bar
SERVING: Lunch & Dinner
PRICE RANGE: $$

Located next to the beach with a décor reminiscent of the deck of a cruise ship. Delicious menu from two chefs offering a wide variety of cuisines – French, European, Mediterranean and Asian dishes. Signature dishes include: Sea bream sashimi marinated in a citrus jus and the famous "Black Cod" marinated in miso. Reservations recommended.

LA TABLE DU CHEF
5, rue Jean Daumas, Cannes, 4-93-68-27-40
CUISINE: Mediterranean, Seafood
DRINKS: Beer & Wine Only
SERVING: Lunch & Dinner
PRICE RANGE: $$
The bossman here, Bruno Gensdarmes, decides what he's serving on a daily basis, so there's no menu. I love places like this because you get to experience something completely surprising. At lunch you get 2 courses, at dinner 4 (soup, fish, meat and dessert). Just Bruno cooking in his claustrophobic kitchen and another one serving in this tiny little spot. Only 15 or 20 tables, so it's small and intimate. Try to get a table outside, but inside's OK, too. Traditional dishes from Provence.

LE BAOLI
Port Pierre Canto, boulevard de la Croisette, Cannes, +33 4 93 43 03 43
www.baolicannes.com
CUISINE: Asian Fusion
DRINKS: Full bar
SERVING: Dinner
PRICE RANGE: $$$$
This is one of the hottest spots in Cannes – part restaurant and part nightclub. Great place for a night out with dinner and dancing. Menu picks: Chilean Sea Bass Heart of Beef Tenderloin. Outdoor dining. Great music – live DJ. Reservations recommended.

LE BACON
664 boulevard de Bacon, Cap d'Antibes, Antibes, 4-93-61-50-02
www.restaurantdebacon.com
CUISINE: Seafood
DRINKS: Full Bar
SERVING: Lunch & Dinner
PRICE RANGE: $$$$
Not far from Cannes is the town of Antibes. It's worth the short trip to take in the panoramic views of the bay from the terrace here. While in Antibes, try out this lovely place (it has one well-deserved Michelin star, having got their first one back in 1979) to get the bouillabaisse. They have several versions of it: with lobster, without lobster, a small "tasting," whatever you like. Don't even think of ordering meat here. You want to focus on the fish, whether it be

bream, chapon, corb, marble, turbot, whatever they are offering. You can count on it being the best.

LE CIRQUE
30 rue Hoche, +33 4 93 30 02 38
www.lecirquecannes.fr
WEBSITE DOWN AT PRESSTIME
CUISINE: Bistro
DRINKS: Full Bar
SERVING: Breakfast, Lunch, & Dinner; Closed Sun
PRICE RANGE: $$$
Popular eatery on a very bust pedestrian street that's usually packed well into the night. If you're lucky, you'll get one of the tables by the street. Simple menu but the food is good. Favorites: Smoked duck breast, Veal chop confit, Lamb, Branzino with braised fennel and Iberian Pork.

LE COUP DE FOURCHETTE
15, Bis Av Charles Dahon, Theoule Sur Mer, 4-93-93-50-05
www.restaurant-le-coup-de-fourchette.fr
CUISINE: Mediterranean, Seafood
DRINKS: Beer & Wine Only
SERVING: Lunch & Dinner
PRICE RANGE: $$
This is another place that's a little bit out of town, but worth the taxi fare. You won't find anything on the menu that's not expertly prepared and efficiently served. I included this place because it's a good example of a small, unpretentious family-run restaurant. It's places like this that explain why French food is so highly valued. Even in the smallest

places, they are award of quality and won't put up with crap. Menu is small, but exquisite, changing with what's fresh. Fish soup with aioli with garlic croutons; sheep's cheeks with sweet potatoes; grilled rabbit; giant prawns; snails; sea bass; duck confit. Tip: sit inside and enjoy watching the chef (who has a lot of pride in his work) behind the counter prepare your food. The terrace outside is OK, but it's right on the street with the traffic.

LE MASCHOU
15, rue St-Antoine, Cannes, 4-93-39-62-21
www.lemaschou.com
CUISINE: Mediterranean
DRINKS: Full Bar
SERVING: Dinner

PRICE RANGE: $$
In the old quarter of Le Suquet you will find this fairly typical spot serving food that's authentic and delicious. Their crudités platter is excellent and all the grilled meats are superb. The Maschou means "nice little house," in a slangy kind of way.

LE PETITE MAISON DE NICOLE
MAJESTIC HOTEL
10 Boulevard de la Croisette, Cannes, +33 4 92 98 77 89
https://www.hotelsbarriere.com/en/cannes/le-majestic.html
CUISINE: French/Vegetarian
DRINKS: Beer & Wine Only
SERVING: Dinner
PRICE RANGE: $$
Beautiful dining experience among original art and vintage chandeliers. Creative menu of French cuisine from Chef Brice Morvent. Menu picks: Fillet of Beef

Rossini style and Scrambled truffles. Live music on Fri & Sat. Popular among celebrities.

LE ROOF
FIVE SEAS HOTEL
1, rue Notre Dame, Cannes, 4-63-36-05-05
www.fiveseashotel.com
CUISINE: Mediterranean
DRINKS: Full Bar
SERVING: Lunch & Dinner
PRICE RANGE: $$
Rooftop place with a good menu and good views.

LE SALON DES INDEPENDANTS
11 Rue Louis Perrissol, 33 4 93 39 97 06
www.le-salon-des-independants-restaurant-cannes.com/
CUISINE: French
DRINKS: Wine
SERVING: Dinner
PRICE RANGE: $$$$
NEIGHBORHOOD: Alpes-Maritimes
Traditional and very elegant and charming, this small French eatery offers an all-inclusive menu – prix fixe - offering fish and a variety of meats. Each customer gets a half-bottle of wine. Favorites: Duck with sweet sauce and Lamb that's succulent and moist. Live music starts at 9 p.m.

LE TUBE
10 Rue Florian, 06400 Cannes, +33 4 93 68 51 69
www.le-tube.com
CUISINE: French/Steakhouse

DRINKS: Full Bar
SERVING: Lunch/Dinner/Late-night
PRICE RANGE: $$$
NEIGHBORHOOD: Cote d'Azur

Located behind the Grand Hotel is this popular upscale steakhouse with an industrial-chic brick wall look that will make you feel like you're in New York rather than the south of France. The barmen are very adept at classic cocktails, which gives it an even stronger feeling of Manhattan. Favorites: premium cuts of beef, the excellent Burrata and Grilled Veal. Impressive wine selection. Indoor & outdoor seating. Great for people watching.

LES TERRAILLERS
11 Chemin Neuf, Biot, +33 4 93 65 01 59
www.lesterraillers.com
CUISINE: French

DRINKS: Full bar
SERVING: Lunch & Dinner; Closed Wed & Thur
PRICE RANGE: $$$$
Somewhat away from the water in charming Biot, Chef Michael Fulci (who worked for Ducasse) offers a varied menu of French cuisine with a touch of Provence. Michelin starred. Indoor dining is lovely but the real experience is dining in the garden complete with grape and Honeysuckle vines. Menu picks: Grilled Swordfish and Filet of Saint-Pierre. Great selection of wines – both local and international. Ideal for a special dinner.

LOUIS XV RESTAURANT
HOTEL DE PARIS MONTECARLO
Place du Casino, Monaco, +377 98 06 88 64
www.hoteldeparismontecarlo.com
CUISINE: French/Mediterranean/European
DRINKS: Full bar
SERVING: Dinner: Thurs – Mon/July & August open for Dinner Wed - Mon

PRICE RANGE: $$$$

As expected from any Alain Ducasse venue, this beautiful restaurant offers an elegant dining experience featuring culinary excellence. Waiters dressed in black suits serve guests that seem like they are dressed for a special occasion and a meal at this restaurant is indeed that. Try to get a table near the French doors so you can see both the gilded room you're in as well as the scene outside the casino. Champagnes, bite-sized h'oeuvres, impressive seafood dishes, breads, and delicious desserts. Wine cellar features some thousands of bottles. Dinner here is truly a memorable experience. If you really want to splurge, get the Pyrenean baby lamb, sprinkled with Espelette pepper.

LUCKY YOU
5 Rue du Dr Pierre Gazagnaire, 33 4 93 68 96 86
www.luckyoucannes.com
CUISINE: Steakhouse, Seafood
DRINKS: Wine
SERVING: Lunch & Dinner
PRICE RANGE: $$$$
NEIGHBORHOOD: Alpes-Maritimes

Quite small, this elegant restaurant offers high-quality meats and seafood, but the emphasis is really on the meats. Burrata with artichokes to start; Pasta with lobster is also a good starter; Spanish filets; Sirloins from Finland; 5 or 6 different rib eye selections; they also have prime rib. Their mashed potatoes are quite famous, so be sure to get a side order. Have a look at the prix fixe menu.

PARK 45
GRAND HÔTEL CANNES
45 Boulevard de la Croisette, Cannes, +33 4 93 38 15 45
grand-hotel-cannes.com/fr
CUISINE: Mediterranean/French
DRINKS: Full bar
SERVING: Lunch & Dinner
PRICE RANGE: $$$$

Chef Sébastien Broda offers a gourmet menu of rich and inventive cuisine in a stunning room with floor-to-ceiling windows offering a dramatic view. Tasting menu or a la carte options. Fresh ingredients, breads baked daily, and excellent Mediterranean cuisine. Set within the Grand Hotel, this is one of Cannes' fashionable beach restaurants. Jude Law eats the sea bass with pistachio nuts here. Wine selection is excellent.

TABLE 22
22 Rue Saint-Antoine-Le-Suquet, Cannes, +33 4 93 39 13 10
www.restaurantmantel.com
CUISINE: French/European/Mediterranean
DRINKS: Full bar
SERVING: Breakfast, Lunch, Dinner and Late Night
PRICE RANGE: $$$$
Located steps from the Palais des Festivals, this eatery offers an impressive menu of gourmet cuisine up in the hilly Le Suquet district. Menu picks: white bean cream soup with white summer truffles, Duck breast and Monk fish. Great choice of pastries and desserts. Here you're waited on hand and foot with 4 waiters to a table.

UVA
13 Boulevard de la Republique, 33 4 93 68 57 01

https://www.facebook.com/UVA-198956247625425/
CUISINE: French, Mediterranean
DRINKS: Full Bar
SERVING: Lunch & Dinner
PRICE RANGE: $$
NEIGHBORHOOD: Le Suquet
Located walking distance from the Cannes strip, this small eatery offers a creative menu of French fare with a strong focus on meats. Favorites: Beef dish (cooked 36 hours) and Risotto with summer truffles. Beautiful housemade desserts. Impressive wine list.

WAZAKURA

13 rue de Bone, Cannes, 93-99-93-42
www.sushibarwazakura.eresto.net
CUISINE: Japanese
DRINKS: Full Bar
SERVING: Lunch & Dinner
PRICE RANGE: $$$
Typical Japanese dishes you can find in most places, but here the quality is superior.

Z PLAGE
Grand Hyatt Cannes Hôtel Martinez
73 Boulevard de la Croisette, Cannes, +33 4 92 98 73 19
https://hotel-martinez.hyatt.com/en/hotel/dining/restaurant-zplage.html

CUISINE: French
DRINKS: Full bar
SERVING: Breakfast, Lunch, Dinner and Late Night
PRICE RANGE: $$$$
Elegant and splashy seaside eatery located in the beautiful Hotel Martinez offering French cuisine and impressive seafood dishes such as Sea Bass and Scallops. Jodie Foster loves this place. Great summer menu and cocktails. Lunch can be served on the beach. Reservations recommended.

Chapter 5
NIGHTLIFE

Whether you're a billionaire mogul in town for a fling, a simple millionaire jet-setter looking for a good time or a backpacker in search of a convivial crowd to share a beer, there's something for you in the pubs, clubs, bars and dives of Cannes.

Everything's not expensive. It's just that the flashiest and showiest places tend to be.

The cobbled alleyways and narrow streets of Le Suquet are where you want to head for that romantic stroll. These streets will bring to mind Woody Allen's "Midnight in Paris."

Something louder, brasher, heart-thumping? Then head over to the rue des Frères Pradignac where you'll locate a string of pulse-pounding bars and smaller clubs.

For entertainment, performing arts listings and other cultural events that will be current with your visit, go to www.cannes.com

BAÔLI
Port Pierre Canto, boulevard de la Croisette, Cannes, 4-93-43-03-43
https://baolicannes.com
Wow! Just what you'd expect from a big-time nightclub in Cannes. (This is where all the stars and other celebs hang out during the film festival, the ones under 50, that is.) Inside the DJs work late into the night. Outside you'll fall in love with the garden, with the drapes flowing in the wind under rustling palm trees while the rich recline on sofas under the

moonlight. Modern decadence at its best. Bring lots of money. (VIPs gain access through a tunnel that snakes under the Croisette, or by a private dock when they come by boat.)

CHARLY'S WINE BAR
5, rue du Suquet, Cannes, +33-6-98-92-40-41
https://www.yelp.com/biz/charlys-wine-cannes?osq=CHARLY%27S+BAR

The place to head to with no cover, but always a groove. It's a big old cave. It's not a snooty place, and all are welcome. Music is insistent without being crazy. A mix of hits from the 1960s through the 1990s with some French pop thrown in for good measure. Draws a well-heeled crowd of all ages.

CLUB BY ALBANE
4 rue de la paix, 75002 Paris, +33 1 42 86 82 08
www.albanecleret.com/en/
Ultra VIP members-only club located on the roof of the JW Marriott.
NEIGHBORHOOD: French Riviera

EST VALLAURI
10, rue des Halles, Cannes, 4-93-68-10-20
No Website
In the Le Suquet section you'll find this good-time wine bar. Quiet and cozy weeknights, they have jazz on the weekends.

GOTHA NIGHTCLUB
Place Franklin Roosevelt, Cannes, +33 4 28 70 20 20

www.gotha-club.com
VIP club with an impressive roster of celebrity performers and DJs. Dress to impress – no sneakers or casual wear. Very popular and usually crowded. Small dance floor.

L'ENDROIT
10, rue du Suquet, Cannes, +33 6 67 76 87 70
No Website
Another great spot in Le Suquet where locals gather is this relaxing wine bar with candles flickering amid the flowers. Here they serve some 35 wines by the glass.

LE 360 LOUNGE BAR
Radisson Blu 1835 Hotel & Thalasso
2, Blvd Jean Hibert, Cannes, 4-92-99-73-10
www.radissonblu.com/hotel-cannes
It's the views of the old harbor, the bay and the surrounding Esterel Hills you want to see from the rooftop lounge here that also serves great food.

LE BAR DES CÉLÉBRITÉS
InterContinental Carlton Hotel
58, Boulevard de la Croisette, Cannes, 04-93-06-40-06
http://www.carlton-cannes.com/fr/gastronomie/carlton-bar/
You'll find lot of cocktail cavaliers tinkling the ivories at the majestic hotels along La Croisette. But you can't go to Cannes without at least walking through the lobby of the Carlton, which is Ground Zero during the film festival in May. If you can afford the steep prices, slip in here at cocktail hour to enjoy the piano bar. What you'll see in here is what you thought glamorous Cannes should be like. Here it is in all its splendor.

LE BROWN SUGAR
17 Rue Frères Pradignac, Cannes, +33 4 93 39 70 10
www.facebook.com/pages/Brown-Sugar-Cannes/505937132760027

This place is popular with the locals. Very welcoming atmosphere, even down to the free bar snacks. It looks like your grandmother's attic with all the junk they have hanging everywhere, from broken bicycles, lanterns, somebody's bet-up saxophone. Very funky. Music is always pumping.

MORRISON'S PUB
10 Rue Teisseire, Cannes, 04-92-98-16-17
www.cannes-nightlife.com/
A sports bar where you'll find a lot of young tourists because the drinks aren't outrageously expensive, the pub fare they serve is really good and the screens are alight with various sports.

Z PLAGE
GRAND HYATT CANNES HÔTEL MARTINEZ
73 Boulevard de la Croisette, Cannes, +33 4 92 98 73 19
https://hotel-martinez.hyatt.com/en/hotel/dining/restaurant-zplage.html
Popular restaurant on the French Riviera that becomes one of the hottest nightspots in Cannes during summer months. Weekends Znight offers concerts, live shows and fireworks.

Chapter 6
WHAT TO SEE & DO

ABBAYE DE LERINS
Île St-Honorat, Cannes, 4-92-99-54-00
www.abbayedelerins.com
We mentioned this place up in the restaurant section. But besides lunch, you should explore the island itself if you have time. The Île St.-Honorat is where the

monks at the monastery make their wine from grapes grown here. You take a ferry from a dock in the Old Port and about 20 minutes later you land on this rugged island. It'll take you a couple of hours to walk around it. You'll see the abandoned medieval abbey, along with other ruins going back centuries. You'll also pass the vineyards. The new abbey has a gift shop where the monks sell their wine.

ÎLE St MARGUERITE
www.cannes.com
This island is reached by taking a ferry as well. It's a wild and beautiful place. In the **Musée de la Mer** you'll see the dungeon where the Man in the Iron Mask was imprisoned.

LA MALMAISON
47, Promenade de la Croisette, Cannes, 4-97-06-44-90
www.cannes.com/fr/culture/centre-d-art-la-malmaison.html
An art museum in one of the loveliest locales in Cannes. Here they mount solo exhibitions of artists from 20th and 21st centuries. Each exhibition gathers about one hundred works from private and public collections for display in the large gallery here.

LE MUSEE BONNARD
16, Boulevard Sadi Carnot, Le Cannet, 4-93-94-06-06
www.museebonnard.fr
Make your way to nearby Le Cannet to see Bonnard's lively landscape paintings of the Riviera, jumping with bright yellows, violets and blues.

MUSÉE DE LA CASTRE
Place de la Castre, Le Suquet, Cannes, 33-04-93-38-55-26
www.culture.gouv.fr/culture/nllefce/fr/mu_06400
At the top of the hill above Cannes, which you reach by climbing up stairs and narrow streets, you'll find this museum noted for its ancient and medieval archeology collections, as well as its non-European ethnography collections (Asia, Oceania, the Americas). More impressive still is the tower dating from the 11th Century that allows you to take in the breathtaking view of the hills rolling down to the sea below, the tiled roofs of the houses, the mountains in the distance. One of the greatest things you'll remember about your visit to Cannes is the view from this tower. Highly recommended that you go out of your way to see it. Modest admission fee.

Chapter 7
SHOPPING & SERVICES

AHIMSA
148, rue Antibes, Cannes, 4-93-43-78-24
www.ahimsacannes.com
WEBSITE DOWN AT PRESSTIME
Great selection of throw pillows in great colors from Africa, hats, loose-fitting shifts, scarves, neckwear,

blankets, jewelry. Unusual collection of shoes for kids.

ALINE BUFFET
Rue de Constantine, Cannes, 93-68-64-51
www.coursalinebuffet.com/
Tailor Fashion Designer Aline Buffet offers exclusive designs made by traditional techniques, the techniques of haute couture and sleight of hand. Every product that comes out of her studio is a work of art that fits perfectly on the female form. She defines her work as metamorphosis and wants women to realize their dream wearing her creations.

AUGUSTIN LATOUR
8, rue Chabaud, Cannes, 4-93-99-08-94
No Website
Tiny little shop not much bigger than your walk-in closet at home, tucked away on a side street, is jam-packed with gifts and accessories for the home. Designers they carry: Tsé & Tsé, Lexon, Galerie Sentou.

BATHROOM GRAFFITI
52, rue d'Antibes, Cannes, 4-93-39-02-32
www.bathroomgraffiti.com
Hundreds of gift items here ranging from plush toys to home accessories, furniture, lamps, items for the kitchen, clothing for men, women and kids, a good assortment of leather goods, lots of deco inspired items.

CAVE RIVIERA
7 Rue Teisseire, Cannes, +33 4 93 38 82 17
No Website
Excellent wine bar and cellar offering fine selection of wines and champagnes. Locals come here because from 5 – 9 the wines are cheaper, and the owner will give you a plate of salami and cheeses. On-site tastings of over 600 varieties.

CHAPELLERIE TESI
56 Rue Meynadier, Cannes, +33 4 93 39 90 65
www.chapellerie-cannes.com
Boutique offering TESI headwear, bags, belts, and scarves but the focus is on hats.

CHEZ PAUL
8 Rue Meynadier, Cannes, 93-38-15-59
www.paul.fr
A French bakery, supplier to the Kings and Queens for over 125 years, with locations reaching 300. The passion of French bread is such an art. They opened really early in the morning, just before sunrise and close at 1.30 in the afternoon. Waking up, I walked from the hotel and had the best croissant ever, along with a café au lait while reading the paper. They also offer a variety of pastries and chocolate croissants, apple croissants and lunch sandwiches.

CHOCOLATIER BRUNO
13 Rue Hoche, Cannes, 93-39-26-63
A beautiful chocolate store on one of those lovely streets good for walking. It is an art like everything else. From the mold to combining the right ingredients. Candies, Confiseries, Truffles, etc. I tasted a few and bought a bag of curried ganache, mocha ganache, vanilla ganache, crème praline, chocolate lavender. They were all very good, not too sweet so I could still taste the bitterness of the chocolate itself. Wonderful selection. Friendly staff.

CINQ MONDES SPA
THE FIVE SEAS HOTEL
1, rue Notre Dame, Cannes, 4-63-36-05-08
www.fiveseashotel.com
Full range of spa services at this nifty new retreat next to the Palais des Festivals.

CIVETTE CARLTON
93 Rue d'Antibes, Cannes, 93-39-55-07
A store featuring not only cigars, but luxury pens as well. Mont Blanc, Cartier, Parker. Centrally located near the Carlton and La Croisette. Here you can find all the brands like Cuban Cohiba, Ashtons, Dunhills and many more. Maduros, Jamaicans, Honduras. A variety of accessories is also available such as cigar cutters, lighters, money clips, wallets, ashtrays. A great big humidor welcomes keeps the cigars in perfect condition. Americans flock here to get "real" Cuban cigars.

FENDI
44 Boulevard de la Croisette, Cannes, +33 4 93 38 05 00
www.fendi.com/us/
Beautiful store decorated similar to the Paris location. Here you will find luxury bags, home collections, jewelry, kidswear, men's shoes, menswear, swimwear, perfumes & fragrances, women's shoes, and womenswear.

FROMAGERIE CENERI
22 Rue Meynadier, Cannes, 93-39-63-68
www.fromagerie-ceneri.com
A dream shop when it comes to cheese. As I entered the freshness and the smell of milk engulfed me. Their private cellar is only two blocks away, where cheeses are stored for aging. Here you can find all your favorites from Brie de Meaux, Camembert,

Reblochon, Gouda, Emmenthaler, Swiss and a unique variety of goat cheeses from firm to soft textures. I sampled Latur, a combination of sheep and goat milk at room temperature, so creamy, delicious on a little crouton or French baguette.

GALERIE DU CARLTON
58 Boulevard La Croisette, Cannes, +33 4 93 06 40 06
http://galerieducarlton.fr
Madame Garnier owns other galleries in Paris and Courchevel, in the French Alps. This particular one is within the InterContinental Carlton and exhibits various artists throughout the year, like Buffet and Novaro for example.

HERMES
52 Boulevard de la Croisette, Cannes, +33 4 93 39 18 23
http://en.stores.hermes.com/Europe/France/Cannes/Hermes-Cannes
Located on the famous Boulevard de la Croisette facing the Mediterranean Sea, this shop features luxury brand products including fashions, handbags, scarves and accessories.

JEAN-LUC PELÉ
36, rue Meynadier, Cannes
42, rue Antibes, Cannes, +33 4 93 38 06 10
Jean-Luc makes the best macaroons and chocolates.

LE MARCHÉ FORVILLE
11 Rue du Marche Forville, Cannes, No Phone
www.marcheforville.com
7:30 am- 12:30 pm
This is the famous "covered market" that runs three blocks. Though it's under a roof, the place is still open-air. There are other markets in Cannes, but nothing like this for the sake of variety and color and lively fun. You can buy most anything here: artisanal olive oils, sausages, jams, meats, produce, fresh herbs, flowers, fruits, vegetables, cheeses, wines, good gift items. They call this market the "belly of Cannes," because this is where people buy a lot of their food. Monday there are not so many sellers of produce, as the place turns into a flea market. It's a

very good idea to spend some time wandering through the streets in this area, because you'll find out how the locals live, see the hardware stores where they buy things, a completely different experience than walking along La Croisette.

LIBRAIRIE ROSSIGNOL
1 rue Jean Daumas, Cannes, 93-39-70-55
www.le-site-de.com/librairie-rossignol-cannes_236657.html
This library shelves are stacked from top to bottom with volumes of beautifully bound rare and antiques books. This shop was founded back in 1928 and has since then built up a hugely impressive collection. M. Rossignol, who is a nationally-renowned book expert, proves to be a fountain of knowledge should you need anything. You can also find music and videos from Edith Piaf to Jean Gabin, Simone Signoret, Yves Montand and many more.

OLIVIER & CO
4 rue Jean Mace, Cannes, 93-39-00-38
www.oliviers-co.com
A Boutique specialized in olive oil based products such as groceries, cosmetics, organic food, just a few to recommend. A variety of different vinegars is also offered like basil and figs or lime honeyed ginger. I bought a can of sardines with sundried tomatoes, a black olive paste with capers and a paste of green olives with anchovies. Since I am a big fan of white truffle oil to ad to pastas, I found just what I was looking for. The prices are great.

PROJECTEURS
135 Rue D'antibes, Cannes, +33 4 93 38 38 04
www.projecteurs-concept.com/en/
Luxury two-level boutique features major designer brands from New York and London. Luxury fashions, jewelry, and accessories. First floor features a tea room serving pastries.

VOG SALON
18 Rue Notre Dame, Cannes, +33 4 93 30 06 41
www.vog.fr/
Specialty hair salon with top hairstylists and colorists. Services include: cut, blow-dry, color, scan, and haircare. One good things is they keep very late hours and also open early.

INDEX

'

'AFFABLE, 26

3

3.14, 15

A

ABBAYE DE LERINS, 57
AHIMSA, 61
AL CHARQ, 22
ALINE BUFFET, 62
Asian Fusion, 36
ASTOUX ET BRUN, 22
AUGUSTIN LATOUR, 62

B

BACON, 36
BAOLI, 50
Bar Grub, 39
BIJOU PLAGE, 24
BUSES, 11

C

CANNELLE, 23
Carlton Beach Restaurant, 12
Carlton Hotel, 53
Carte 10 pass, 11
CAVE RIVIERA, 63
CHAPELLERIE TESI, 64
CHARLY'S WINE BAR, 51
CHATEAU SAINT-MARTIN, 13
CHEZ PAUL, 64
CHOCOLATIER BRUNO, 65
CINQ MONDES SPA, 65
CIVETTE CARLTON, 65
CLUB BY ALBANE, 51
COLOMBE D'OR, 30
COSY BOX, 24
COUP DE FOURCHETTE, 37
CRESCI, 24

E

ET VALLAURI, 51
European, 28, 34, 42, 45

F

FENDI'S, 66
FIVE SEAS HOTEL, 14, 65
French, 28, 34, 41, 42, 44, 45, 48
FROMAGERIE CENERI, 66

G

GALERIE DU CARLTON, 67
GASTON ET GASTOUNETTE, 25
GOTHA NIGHTCLUB, 51
GRAFFITI, 63
GRAND HÔTEL CANNES, 44
GRAND HYATT CANNES HÔTEL MARTINEZ, 47, 54
GRILL & WINES, 26

H

HERMES, 67
HOTEL BARRIERE, 34
HOTEL BARRIERE LE MAJESTIC, 15
HOTEL DE PARIS MONTECARLO, 42
HOTEL DU CAP-EDEN ROC, 17
HOTEL LE CANBERRA, 18
Hotel Martinez, 33

I

Île St-Honorat, 57
Italian, 24, 27, 28, 29, 31, 33, 37

J

JEAN-LUC PELE, 68

L

L'ASSIETTE PROVENCALE, 27
L'AME, 27
L'ECRIN, 28
L'ENDROIT, 52
L'ONDINE PIAGE, 28
LA BROUETTE DE GRAND-MERE, 28
LA CASA DI NONNA, 29
LA CAVE, 29
LA GUERITE, 31
LA MALMAISON, 59
LA MEISSOUNIERE, 32
LA MOME, 33
LA PALME D'OR, 33
LA PLAGE RESTAURANT, 34
LE 360 LOUNGE BAR, 52
LE BAOLI, 36
LE BAR DES CÉLÉBRITÉS, 53
LE BROWN SUGAR, 53
Le Café Blanc, 18
LE CIRQUE, 37
LE MARCHE FORVILLE, 68
LE MUSEE BONNARD, 59
LE PETITE MAISON DE NICOLE, 39

LE SALON DES INDEPENDANTS, 40
LE TUBE, 40
Lebanese, 22
LES TERRAILLERS, 41
LIBERA, 32
LOUIS XV RESTAURANT, 42
LUCKY YOU, 43

M

MAJESTIC HOTEL, 39
MARGUERITE, 58
MASCHOU, 38
Mediterranean, 28, 34, 42, 44, 45
MORRISON'S PUB, 54
MUSEE DE LA CASTRE, 60
Musée de la Mer, 58

O

OLIVIER & CO, 69

P

PARK 45, 44
PROJECTEURS, 70
PRULY, 18

R

Radisson Blu, 52
RADISSON BLU 1835 HOTEL, 19

ROSSIGNOL, 69

S

SALON DE GOURMANDISES, 14
SEA SENS, 14
Seafood, 23, 28

T

TABLE DU CHEF, 35
TAXIS, 11
Taxis de Cannes, 11

U

UVA, 45

V

VILLA GABRES HOTEL, 16
Villa Garbo, 16
VOG SALON, 70

W

WAZAKURA, 46

Z

Z PLAGE, 47, 54

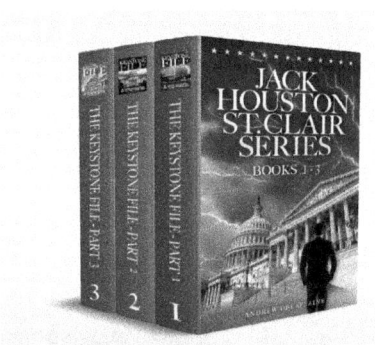

WANT 3 FREE THRILLERS?

Why, of course you do!

If you like these writers--
Vince Flynn, Brad Thor, Tom Clancy, James Patterson, David Baldacci, John Grisham, Brad Meltzer, Daniel Silva, Don DeLillo

If you like these TV series –
House of Cards, Scandal, West Wing, The Good Wife, Madam Secretary, Designated Survivor

You'll love the **unputdownable** series about Jack Houston St. Clair, with political intrigue, romance, suspense.

Besides writing travel books, I've written political thrillers for many years that have delighted hundreds of thousands of readers. I want to introduce you to my work!
Send me an email and I'll send you a link where you can download the first 3 books in my bestselling series,

absolutely FREE.

Mention **this book** when you email me.

andrewdelaplaine@mac.com

www.ingramcontent.com/pod-product-compliance
Lightning Source LLC
Chambersburg PA
CBHW061506040426
42450CB00008B/1499